Sugar and spice and everything nice…that's what these sets are made of! Doesn't this look like a fun photo shoot? It's not every day that we're surrounded by candy and lollipops but maybe it should be. I'm sure the world would be a happier place if we all had one required lollipop a day. Until that happens, we'll all just have to enjoy creating the perfect set for our favorite little misses. One of these sweaters is sure to suit her and what outfit is complete without a matching cap? Whether she's bold and bright or soft and sweet, you can mix up just the right match with a great yarn and just a little time. In fact, these are easy enough that you don't have to stop with just one! Sweet or spicy, I'd love to see how your mixture turns out! Please snap a picture and send to me at **KnitCrochetEditor@leisurearts.com**.

Cheryl

Cheryl Johnson
Knit & Crochet Publication Director

P.S. If you'd like to find out more about what I'm working on, life behind the scenes here at Leisure Arts, or sneak peeks of new publications, check out my blog at http://livinginamaterialworld.blogspot.com.

lots of love baby wear

I0879203

Leisure Arts Inc.
Little Rock, Arkansas

Cap

Shown on page 3.

INTERMEDIATE

Size	Head Circumference
Infant	15" (38 cm)
Toddler	17" (43 cm)

Size Note: Instructions are written for Infant size with Toddler size in braces { }. Instructions will be easier to read if you circle all the numbers pertaining to your child's size. If only one number is given, it applies to both sizes.

MATERIALS

MEDIUM 4

Medium Weight Yarn
[6 ounces, 330 yards (170 grams, 302 meters) per skein]: 1 skein
Straight knitting needles, size 8 (5 mm) **or** size needed for gauge
Yarn needle

GAUGE: In Stockinette Stitch,
18 sts and 24 rows = 4" (10 cm)

Note: When instructed to slip a stitch, slip it as if to **knit**.

CROWN

Cast on 6 sts.

Row 1 (Right side)**:** Increase by knitting into the front **and** into the back of each st across ***(Figs. 2a & b, page 18)***: 12 sts.

Row 2: Purl across.

Row 3: Knit across.

Row 4: Purl across.

Row 5 (Increase row)**:** [K1, M1 ***(Figs. 3a & b, page 18)***] across to last st, K1: 23 sts.

Rows 6-9: Repeat Rows 2-5: 45 sts.

Rows 10-14: Repeat Rows 2 and 3 twice, then repeat Row 2 once **more**.

Row 15: (K3, M1) twice, (K4, M1) 8 times, (K3, M1) twice, K1: 57 sts.

Rows 16 thru 20{22}: Repeat Rows 2 and 3, 2{3} times, then repeat Row 2 once **more**.

TODDLER SIZE ONLY

Row 23: (K7, M1) across to last st, K1: 65 sts.

Row 24: Purl across

BRIM

Rows 1-4: Knit across.

Row 5: K 25{29}, YO ***(Fig. 1, page 18)***, SSK ***(Figs. 6a-c, page 19)***, K3, K2 tog ***(Fig. 5, page 19)***, YO, knit across.

Row 6: K 25{29}, P2, K3, P2, knit across.

Row 7: K 23{27}, † K2 tog, YO, K1, YO, SSK †, K1, repeat from † to † once, knit across.

Row 8: K 24{28}, P4, K1, P4, knit across.

Row 9: K 22{26}, K2 tog, YO, K3, YO, [slip 1, K2 tog, PSSO ***(Figs. 7a & b, page 19)***], YO, K3, YO, SSK, knit across.

Row 10: K 23{27}, P 11, knit across.

Row 11: K 21{25}, K2 tog, YO, K 11, YO, SSK, knit across.

Row 12: K 22{26}, P 13, knit across.

Row 13: K 23{27}, YO, SSK, K7, K2 tog, YO, knit across.

Row 14: K 23{27}, P 11, knit across.

Row 15: K 24{28}, YO, SSK, K5, K2 tog, YO, knit across.

Row 16: K 24{28}, P9, knit across.

Row 17: K 25{29}, YO, SSK, K3, K2 tog, YO, knit across.

Row 18: K 25{29}, P7, knit across.

Row 19: K 26{30}, YO, SSK, K1, K2 tog, YO, knit across.

Row 20: K 26{30}, P5, knit across.

Row 21: K 27{31}, YO, slip 1, K2 tog, PSSO, YO, knit across.

Rows 22-24: Knit across.

Bind off all sts in **knit** leaving long end for sewing.

Thread needle with long end and sew seam, gathering cast on sts at top. Secure end.

Hat
with Turned up Brim

Version A shown on page 5. Version B shown on front cover.

INTERMEDIATE

Size	**Head Circumference**
Toddler	19"-20" (48.5 cm - 51 cm)

MATERIALS

MEDIUM 4

Medium Weight Yarn
[6 ounces, 330 yards
(170 grams, 302 meters) per skein]:
Version A
Blue - 1 skein
Version B
Blue - 1 skein
Green - 1 skein
16" (40.5 cm) Circular knitting needle,
size 8 (5 mm) **or** size needed for gauge
Double pointed needles, size 8 (5 mm)
Marker
Yarn needle

GAUGE: In Stockinette Stitch,
18 sts and 24 rows = 4" (10 cm)

Note: When instructed to slip a stitch, slip it as if to **knit**.

BRIM

With circular knitting needle and Blue, cast on 80 sts ***(see Circular Knitting, page 20)***, place marker to mark beginning of rnd ***(see Markers, page 18)***.

Rnd 1 (Right side)**:** Knit around.

Rnd 2: Purl around.

Rnds 3 and 4: Repeat Rnds 1 and 2.

Rnd 5: K5, ★ † YO ***(Fig. 1, page 18)***, SSK ***(Figs. 6a-c, page 19)***, K3, K2 tog ***(Fig. 5, page 19)***, YO †, K9; repeat from ★ 3 times **more**, then repeat from † to † once, K4.

Rnd 6: P5, K2, P3, K2, (P9, K2, P3, K2) 4 times, P4.

Rnd 7: K3, ★ † K2 tog, YO, K1, YO, SSK, K1, K2 tog, YO, K1, YO, SSK †, K5; repeat from ★ 3 times **more**, then repeat from † to † once, K2.

Rnd 8: P4, K4, P1, K4, (P7, K4, P1, K4) 4 times, P3.

Rnd 9: K2, ★ † K2 tog, YO, K3, YO, [slip 1, K2 tog, PSSO ***(Figs. 7a & b, page 19)***], YO, K3, YO, SSK †, K3; repeat from ★ 3 times **more**, then repeat from † to † once, K1.

Rnd 10: P3, K 11, (P5, K 11) 4 times, P2.

Rnd 11: (K1, K2 tog, YO, K 11, YO, SSK) 5 times.

Rnd 12: P2, K 13, (P3, K 13) 4 times, P1.

Rnd 13: K3, YO, SSK, K7, K2 tog, (YO, K5, YO, SSK, K7, K2 tog) 4 times, YO, K2.

Rnd 14: P3, K 11, (P5, K 11) 4 times, P2.

Rnd 15: K4, YO, SSK, K5, K2 tog, (YO, K7, YO, SSK, K5, K2 tog) 4 times, YO, K3.

Rnd 16: P4, K9, (P7, K9) 4 times, P3.

Rnd 17: K5, YO, SSK, K3, K2 tog, (YO, K9, YO, SSK, K3, K2 tog) 4 times, YO, K4.

Rnd 18: P5, K7, (P9, K7) 4 times, P4.

Rnd 19: K6, YO, SSK, K1, K2 tog, (YO, K 11, YO, SSK, K1, K2 tog) 4 times, YO, K5.

Rnd 20: P6, K5, (P 11, K5) 4 times, P5.

Rnd 21: K7, YO, slip 1, K2 tog, PSSO, (YO, K 13, YO, slip 1, K2 tog, PSSO) 4 times, YO, K6.

Rnd 22: Purl around.

Rnd 23: Knit around.

CROWN

Turn Brim **wrong** side out. Your yarn is now in position as if to **purl**. Slip first st on right needle to left needle. Bring yarn back between needles in position as if to **knit**. Slip same stitch from left needle back to right needle. Stitch is now wrapped.

Rnd 1: Knit around to last st (wrapped st), knit wrap and the st it wraps together ***(Fig. A)***.

Fig. A

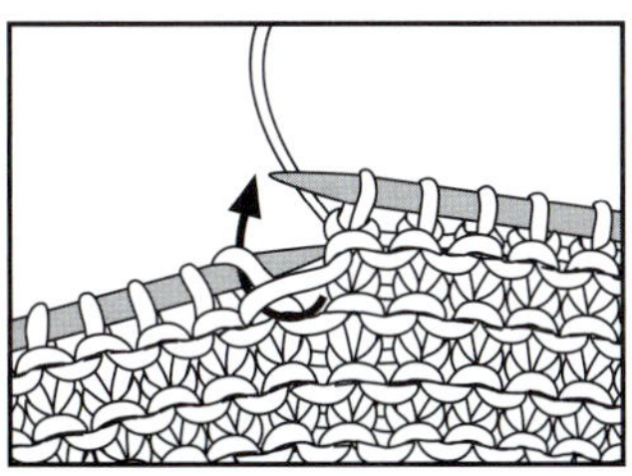

For Version A, continue working in Blue. For Version B, cut Blue and change to Green at beginning of Rnd 6.

Rnds 2-6: Knit around.

Rnds 7-16: (K2, P2) around.

Rnds 17-25: Knit around.

Change to double pointed needles when sts will no longer fit on circular needle.

Rnd 26: (K6, K2 tog) around: 70 sts.

Rnds 27-29: Knit around.

Rnd 30: (K5, K2 tog) around: 60 sts.

Rnds 31-33: Knit around.

Rnd 34: (K4, K2 tog) around: 50 sts.

Rnds 35 and 36: Knit around.

Rnd 37: (K3, K2 tog) around: 40 sts.

Rnds 38 and 39: Knit around.

Rnd 40: (K2, K2 tog) around: 30 sts.

Rnd 41: Knit around.

Rnd 42: (K1, K2 tog) around: 20 sts.

Rnd 43: K2 tog around; cut yarn leaving long end for weaving: 10 sts.

Thread needle with long end, then weave needle through remaining sts on Rnd 43. Gather **tightly** and secure end. Turn Brim up.

Blanket

Shown on page 7.

INTERMEDIATE

Finished Size: 35" x 45" (89 cm x 114.5 cm)

MATERIALS

MEDIUM 4

Medium Weight Yarn
[6 ounces, 330 yards
(170 grams, 302 meters) per skein]:
4 skeins
29" (73.5 cm) Circular knitting needle,
size 10 (6 mm) **or** size needed for gauge

GAUGE: In Stockinette Stitch,
16 sts and 20 rows = 4" (10 cm)

Note: When instructed to slip a stitch, slip it as if to **knit**.

BLANKET

Cast on 141 sts.

Rows 1-10: Knit across.

Row 11 (Right side)**:** K5, YO ***(Fig. 1, page 18)***, K2 tog ***(Fig. 5, page 19)***, K1, (YO, K2 tog) across to last 7 sts, SSK ***(Figs. 6a-c, page 19)***, YO, K5.

Row 12: Knit across.

Row 13: K5, YO, K2 tog, knit across to last 7 sts, SSK, YO, K5.

Row 14: K7, purl across to last 7 sts, K7.

Rows 15-19: Repeat Rows 13 and 14 twice, then repeat Row 13 once **more**.

Row 20: Knit across.

Row 21: Repeat Row 13.

Row 22: Knit across.

Row 23: K5, YO, K2 tog, K6, ★ † YO, SSK, K3, K2 tog †, YO, K 11; repeat from ★ 5 times **more**, then repeat from † to † once, YO, K6, SSK, YO, K5.

Row 24: K 13, P2, K3, P2, (K 11, P2, K3, P2) 6 times, K 13.

Row 25: K5, YO, K2 tog, K4, ★ † K2 tog, YO, K1, YO, SSK, K1, K2 tog, YO, K1, YO, SSK †, K7; repeat from ★ 5 times **more**, then repeat from † to † once, K4, SSK, YO, K5.

Row 26: K 12, P4, K1, P4, (K9, P4, K1, P4) 6 times, K 12.

Row 27: K5, YO, K2 tog, K3, ★ † K2 tog, YO, K3, YO, [slip 1, K2 tog, PSSO ***(Figs. 7a & b, page 19)***], YO, K3, YO, SSK †, K5; repeat from ★ 5 times **more**, then repeat from † to † once, K3, SSK, YO, K5.

Row 28: K 11, P 11, (K7, P 11) 6 times, K 11.

Row 29: K5, YO, K2 tog, K2, ★ † K2 tog, YO, K 11, YO, SSK †, K3; repeat from ★ 5 times **more**, then repeat from † to † once, K2, SSK, YO, K5.

Row 30: K 10, P 13, (K5, P 13) 6 times, K 10.

Row 31: K5, YO, K2 tog, K4, ★ † YO, SSK, K7, K2 tog †, YO, K7; repeat from ★ 5 times **more**, then repeat from † to † once, YO, K4, SSK, YO, K5.

Row 32: K 11, P 11, (K7, P 11) 6 times, K 11.

Row 33: K5, YO, K2 tog, K5, ★ † YO, SSK, K5, K2 tog †, YO, K9; repeat from ★ 5 times **more**, then repeat from † to † once, YO, K5, SSK, YO, K5.

Row 34: K 12, P9, (K9, P9) 6 times, K 12.

Row 35: K5, YO, K2 tog, K6, ★ † YO, SSK, K3, K2 tog †, YO, K 11; repeat from ★ 5 times **more**, then repeat from † to † once, YO, K6, SSK, YO, K5.

Row 36: K 13, P7, (K 11, P7) 6 times, K 13.

Row 37: K5, YO, K2 tog, K7, ★ † YO, SSK, K1, K2 tog †, YO, K 13; repeat from ★ 5 times **more**, then repeat from † to † once, YO, K7, SSK, YO, K5.

Row 38: K 14, P5, (K 13, P5) 6 times, K 14.

Row 39: K5, YO, K2 tog, K8, ★ † YO, slip 1, K2 tog, PSSO †, YO, K 15; repeat from ★ 5 times **more**, then repeat from † to † once YO, K8, SSK, YO, K5.

Row 40: Knit across.

Row 41: K5, YO, K2 tog, knit across to last 7 sts, SSK, YO, K5.

Row 42: Knit across.

Row 43: K5, YO, K2 tog, knit across to last 7 sts, SSK, YO, K5.

Row 44: K7, purl across to last 7 sts, K7.

Rows 45-49: Repeat Rows 43 and 44 twice, then repeat Row 43 once **more**.

Row 50: Knit across.

Rows 51-290: Repeat Rows 11-50, 6 times.

Row 291: K5, YO, K2 tog, K1, (YO, K2 tog) across to last 7 sts, SSK, YO, K5.

Rows 292-301: Knit across.

Bind off all sts in **knit**.

Baby Cardigan

Shown on page 9.

INTERMEDIATE

Size	Finished Chest Measurement
6 months	$22^{1}/_{4}$" (56.5 cm)
12 months	$24^{1}/_{4}$" (61.5 cm)

Size Note: Instructions are written for size 6 months with size 12 months in braces { }. Instructions will be easier to read if you circle all the numbers pertaining to your child's size. If only one number is given, it applies to both sizes.

MATERIALS

MEDIUM 4

- Medium Weight Yarn
  - [6 ounces, 330 yards
    - (170 grams, 302 meters) per skein]:
      - 1{2} skein(s)
- Straight knitting needles, size 8 (5 mm) **or** size needed for gauge
- Crochet hook, size G (4 mm)
- Yarn needle

GAUGE: In Garter Stitch,
17 sts and 34 rows = 4" (10 cm)

STITCH GUIDE

CHAIN

To work a chain stitch, begin with a slip knot on the hook. Bring the yarn **over** hook from back to front, catching the yarn with the hook and turning the hook slightly toward you to keep the yarn from slipping off. Draw the yarn through the slip knot ***(Fig. A)***.

Fig. A

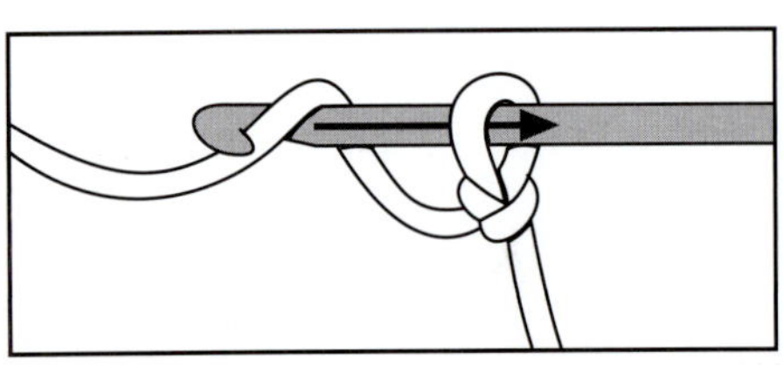

Each piece is worked from the top down.

Note: When instructed to slip a stitch, slip it as if to **knit**.

BACK

Cast on 49{53} sts.

Row 1: Knit across.

Row 2 (Right side)**:** Knit across.

Continue in Garter Stitch (knit every row) until Back measures approximately $9^{1}/_{2}${10}"/24{25.5} cm from cast on edge, ending by working a **wrong** side row.

Eyelet Row: K2, YO ***(Fig. 1, page 18)***, K2 tog ***(Fig. 5, page 19)***, (YO, K2 tog) across to last st, K1.

Last Row: Knit across.

Bind off all sts in **knit**.

RIGHT FRONT

Cast on 15{17} sts.

Row 1: Knit across.

Row 2 (Right side)**:** Knit across.

Rows 3 thru 7{13}: Knit across.

NECK SHAPING

Row 1 (Increase row)**:** Knit across to last st, increase by knitting into the front **and** back of last st ***(Figs. 2a & b, page 18)***: 16{18} sts.

Row 2: Knit across.

Rows 3-6: Repeat Rows 1 and 2 twice: 18{20} sts.

Row 7: Knit across, **turn**; add on 7 sts ***(Figs. 4a & b, page 18)***: 25{27} sts.

Work even in Garter Stitch until Right Front measures approximately 6{6$^1/_2$}"/15{16.5} cm from cast on edge, ending by working a **wrong** side row.

HEART MOTIF

Row 1: K9{10}, YO, SSK ***(Figs. 6a-c, page 19)***, K3, K2 tog, YO, K9{10}.

Row 2: K9{10}, P2, K3, P2, K9{10}.

Row 3: K7{8}, K2 tog, YO, K1, YO, SSK, K1, K2 tog, YO, K1, YO, SSK, K7{8}.

Row 4: K8{9}, P4, K1, P4, K8{9}.

Row 5: K6{7}, K2 tog, YO, K3, YO, [slip 1, K2 tog, PSSO ***(Figs. 7a & b, page 19)***], YO, K3, YO, SSK, K6{7}.

Row 6: K7{8}, P 11, K7{8}.

Row 7: K5{6}, K2 tog, YO, K 11, YO, SSK, K5{6}.

Row 8: K6{7}, P 13, K6{7}.

Row 9: K7{8}, YO, SSK, K7, K2 tog, YO, K7{8}.

Row 10: K7{8}, P 11, K7{8}.

Row 11: K8{9}, YO, SSK, K5, K2 tog, YO, K8{9}.

Row 12: K8{9}, P9, K8{9}.

Row 13: K9{10}, YO, SSK, K3, K2 tog, YO, K9{10}.

Row 14: K9{10}, P7, K9{10}.

Row 15: K 10{11}, YO, SSK, K1, K2 tog, YO, K 10{11}.

Row 16: K 10{11}, P5, K 10{11}.

Row 17: K 11{12}, YO, slip 1, K2 tog, PSSO, YO, K 11{12}.

Continue in Garter Stitch until Right Front measures approximately 9$^1/_2${10}"/24{25.5} cm from cast on edge, ending by working a **wrong** side row.

Eyelet Row: K2, (YO, K2 tog) across to last st, K1.

Last Row: Knit across.

Bind off all sts in **knit**.

Instructions continued on page 10.

LEFT FRONT

Cast on 15{17} sts.

Row 1: Knit across.

Row 2 (Right side)**:** Knit across.

Rows 3 thru 7{13}: Knit across.

NECK SHAPING

Row 1 (Increase row)**:** Increase, knit across: 16{18} sts.

Row 2: Knit across.

Rows 3-6: Repeat Rows 1 and 2 twice: 18{20} sts.

Row 7: Add on 7 sts, knit across: 25{27} sts.

Work even in Garter Stitch until Left Front measures approximately 6{6 1/2}"/15{16.5} cm from cast on edge, ending by working a **wrong** side row.

Beginning with Heart Motif, complete same as Right Front.

SLEEVE (Make 2)

Cast on 39{41} sts.

Row 1: Knit across.

Row 2 (Right side)**:** Knit across.

Continue in Garter Stitch until Sleeve measures approximately 6{6 1/2}"/15{16.5} cm from cast on edge, ending by working a **wrong** side row.

Eyelet Row: K2, (YO, K2 tog) across to last st, K1.

Last Row: Knit across.

Bind off all sts in **knit**.

NECK TIE (Make 2)

With crochet hook, make a chain approximately 9" (23 cm) long; finish off.

FINISHING

Sew shoulder seams.

Sew Sleeves to Sweater, matching center of cast on edge of Sleeve to shoulder seam and beginning 4 1/2{4 3/4}"/11.5{12} cm down from seam.

Sew underarm and side in one continuous seam.

Sew one Neck Tie to each corner of Front Neck.

Boatneck Pullover

EASY

Size	Finished Chest Measurement
2	25" (63.5 cm)
4	27" (68.5 cm)
6	28$^{3}/_{4}$" (73 cm)

Size Note: Instructions are written for size 2 with sizes 4 and 6 in braces { }. Instructions will be easier to read if you circle all the numbers pertaining to your child's size. If only one number is given, it applies to all sizes.

MATERIALS

Medium Weight Yarn (MEDIUM 4)
[6 ounces, 330 yards (170 grams, 302 meters) per skein]:
2{2-3} skeins
Straight knitting needles, size 9 (6.5 mm) **or** size needed for gauge
Markers
Yarn needle
$^{3}/_{4}$" (19 mm) Buttons - 2

GAUGE: In Stockinette Stitch (knit one row, purl one row), 17 sts and 24 rows = 4" (10 cm)

Back and Front are worked from the top down.

Note: When instructed to slip a stitch, slip it as if to **knit**.

BACK

YOKE

Cast on 53{57-61} sts.

Row 1: Knit across.

Row 2 (Right side)**:** Knit across.

Continue in Garter Stitch (knit every row) until Yoke measures approximately 6{7-7$^{1}/_{2}$}"/15{18-19} cm from cast on edge, ending by working a **wrong** side row.

BODY

Increase Row: K1, M1 ***(Figs. 3a & b, page 18)***, knit across to last st, M1, K1: 55{59-63} sts.

Place markers in each end of Increase Row for Sleeve placement.

Instructions continued on page 12.

Beginning with a **purl** row, work in Stockinette Stitch until Body measures approximately $5^{1}/_{2}${$6^{1}/_{2}$-7}"/29{34.5-18} cm from cast on edge, ending by working a **purl** row.

Decrease Row: K1, SSK ***(Figs. 6a-c, page 19)***, knit across to last 3 sts, K2 tog ***(Fig. 5, page 19)***, K1: 53{57-61} sts.

Last 11{15-15} Rows: Knit across.

Bind off all sts in **knit**.

FRONT

YOKE

Cast on 53{57-61} sts.

Rows 1-5: Knit across.

Row 6 (Right side - Buttonhole row)**:** K 12{12-14}, YO ***(Fig. 1, page 18)***, K2 tog, K 25{29-29}, SSK, YO, knit across.

Rows 7-11: Knit across.

Row 12: K 23{25-27}, YO, SSK, K3, K2 tog, YO, knit across.

Row 13: K 23{25-27}, P2, K3, P2, knit across.

Row 14: K 21{23-25}, K2 tog, YO, K1, YO, SSK, K1, K2 tog, YO, K1, YO, SSK, knit across.

Row 15: K 22{24-26}, P4, K1, P4, knit across.

Row 16: K 20{22-24}, K2 tog, YO, K3, YO, [slip 1, K2 tog, PSSO ***(Figs. 7a & b, page 19)***], YO, K3, YO, SSK, knit across.

Row 17: K 21{23-25}, P 11, knit across.

Row 18: K 19{21-23}, K2 tog, YO, K 11, YO, SSK, knit across.

Row 19: K 20{22-24}, P 13, knit across.

Row 20: K 21{23-25}, YO, SSK, K7, K2 tog, YO, knit across.

Row 21: K 21{23-25}, P 11, knit across.

Row 22: K 22{24-26}, YO, SSK, K5, K2 tog, YO, knit across.

Row 23: K 22{24-26}, P9, knit across.

Row 24: K 23{25-27}, YO, SSK, K3, K2 tog, YO, knit across.

Row 25: K 23{25-27}, P7, knit across.

Row 26: K 24{26-28}, YO, SSK, K1, K2 tog, YO, knit across.

Row 27: K 24{26-28}, P5, knit across.

Row 28: K 25{27-29}, YO, slip 1, K2 tog, PSSO, YO, knit across.

Work in Garter Stitch until Yoke measures approximately 5{6-6$^1/_2$}"/12.5{15-16.5} cm from cast on edge, ending by working a **wrong** side row.

BODY

Beginning with Increase Row, complete same as Back.

SLEEVE (Make 2)

Cast on 24{28-30} sts.

Rows 1 thru 11{15-15}: Knit across.

Row 12{16-16} (Right side)**:** [K5{6-6}, M1] 4 times, K4{4-6}: 28{32-34} sts.

Row 13{17-17}: Purl across.

Row 14{18-18}: Increase ***(Figs. 2a & b, page 18)***, knit across to last st, increase: 30{34-36} sts.

Working in Stockinette Stitch, continue to increase one stitch at **each** edge in same manner, every other row, 2{1-1} time(s); then increase every fourth row, 5{9-10} times: 44{54-58} sts.

Work even until Sleeve measures approximately 7{10-11}"/18{25.5-28} cm from cast on edge, ending by working a **purl** row.

Bind off all sts in **knit**.

FINISHING

With **right** sides facing and shoulder edges together, overlap Front over Back by 1" (2.5 cm). Beginning at armhole edge, sew left Front shoulder to Back for 1$^1/_2$ {1$^1/_2$-2}"/4{4-5} cm.

Repeat for right Front shoulder.

Sew Sleeves to Sweater, matching center of last row of Sleeve to shoulder seam and side edges to marked rows.

Sew underarm and side in one continuous seam leaving last 11(15-15) rows unsown for side slit.

Sew a button to each Back shoulder opposite buttonhole on Front shoulder.

Top Down Raglan

Shown on page 15.

INTERMEDIATE

Size	Finished Chest Measurement
2	24" (61 cm)
4	26" (66 cm)
6	27 1/2" (70 cm)

Size Note: Instructions are written for size 2 with sizes 4 and 6 in braces { }. Instructions will be easier to read if you circle all the numbers pertaining to your child's size. If only one number is given, it applies to all sizes.

MATERIALS

MEDIUM 4

Medium Weight Yarn
[6 ounces, 330 yards
(170 grams, 302 meters) per skein]:
2 {2-3} skeins
16" (40.5 cm) **and** 24" (61 cm) Circular knitting needles, size 8 (5 mm) **or** size needed for gauge
Double pointed needles (set of 4), size 7 (4.5 mm)
Markers
Stitch holders - 2
Yarn needle

GAUGE: In Stockinette Stitch,
18 sts and 25 rows = 4" (10 cm)

Note: When instructed to slip a stitch, slip it as if to **knit**.

NECK AND RAGLAN SHAPING

With double pointed knitting needles, cast on 52{52-68} sts ***(see Circular Knitting, page 20)***, place marker to mark beginning of rnd ***(see Markers, page 18)***.

Rnd 1: Knit around.**Rnd 2:** Purl around.

Rnds 3-6: Repeat Rnds 1 and 2 twice.

Rnd 7: K1, place marker, K 18{18-24} for Front, place marker, K1, place marker, K6{6-8} for Sleeve, place marker, K1, place marker, K 18{18-24} for Back, place marker, K1, place marker, K6{6-8} for Sleeve.

Rnd 8 (Increase rnd)**:** ★ K1, slip marker, M1 ***(Figs. 3a & b, page 18)***, knit across to next marker, M1, slip marker; repeat from ★ 3 times **more**: 60{60-76} sts.

Continuing in Stockinette Stitch (knit every rnd) and changing to circular needle as stitch count increases, continue to increase in same manner, every other rnd, 11{11-9} times; then increase every fourth rnd, 1{3-4} time(s): 156{172-180} sts.

Work even until Sweater measures approximately 6{7 1/4-7 1/2}"/15{18.5-19} cm from cast on edge.

BODY

When working Dividing Rnd, remove all markers.

Dividing Rnd: K 46{50-54}, slip next 32{36-36} sts onto st holder for Sleeve, **turn**, add on 8 sts for underarm ***(Figs. 4a & b, page 18)***, **turn**, K 46{50-54}, slip next 32{36-36} sts onto st holder for Sleeve, **turn**, add on 4 sts, place a marker to mark beginning of rnd, add on 4 sts, **turn**: 108{116-124} sts.

Work even until Body measures approximately 1 1/2{3 1/2-3 1/2}"/4{9-9} cm from Dividing Rnd.

Next Rnd: [P 52{56-60}, P2 tog ***(Fig. 8, page 19)***] twice: 106{114-122} sts.

HEART PANEL

Rnd 1: [YO ***(Fig. 1, page 18)***, K2 tog ***(Fig. 5, page 19)***] around.

Rnd 2: Purl around.

Rnds 3-9: Knit around.

Rnd 10: Purl around.

Rnd 11: Knit around.

Rnd 12: Purl around.

Rnd 13: K7{9-11}, YO, SSK ***(Figs. 6a-c, page 19)***, K3, K2 tog, YO, † K9, YO, SSK, K3, K2 tog, YO †; repeat from † to † once **more**, K 14{18-22}, YO, SSK, K3, K2 tog, YO, repeat from † to † twice, K7{9-11}.

Rnd 14: P7{9-11}, K2, P3, K2, † P9, K2, P3, K2 †; repeat from † to † once **more**, P 14{18-22}, K2, P3, K2, repeat from † to † twice, P7{9-11}.

Rnd 15: K5{7-9}, K2 tog, YO, K1, YO, SSK, K1, K2 tog, YO, K1, YO, SSK, † K5, K2 tog, YO, K1, YO, SSK, K1, K2 tog, YO, K1, YO, SSK †; repeat from † to † once **more**, K 10{14-18}, K2 tog, YO, K1, YO, SSK, K1, K2 tog, YO, K1, YO, SSK, repeat from † to † twice, K5{7-9}.

Rnd 16: P6{8-10}, K4, P1, K4, † P7, K4, P1, K4 †; repeat from † to † once **more**, P 12{16-20}, K4, P1, K4, repeat from † to † twice, P6{8-10}.

Rnd 17: K4{6-8}, K2 tog, YO, K3, YO, [slip 1, K2 tog, PSSO ***(Figs. 7a & b, page 19)***], YO, K3, YO, SSK, † K3, K2 tog, YO, K3, YO, slip 1, K2 tog, PSSO, YO, K3, YO, SSK †; repeat from † to † once **more**, K8{12-16}, K2 tog, YO, K3, YO, slip 1, K2 tog, PSSO, YO, K3, YO, SSK, repeat from † to † twice, K4{6-8}.

Rnd 18: P5{7-9}, K 11, (P5, K 11) twice, P 10{14-18}, K 11, (P5, K 11) twice, P5{7-9}.

Rnd 19: K3{5-7}, † K2 tog, YO, K 11, YO, SSK, (K1, K2 tog, YO, K 11, YO, SSK) twice †, K6{10-14}, repeat from † to † once, K3{5-7}.

Rnd 20: P4{6-8}, K 13, (P3, K 13) twice, P8{12-16}, K 13, (P3, K 13) twice, P4{6-8}.

Rnd 21: K5{7-9}, † YO, SSK, K7, K2 tog, (YO, K5, YO, SSK, K7, K2 tog) twice, YO †, K 10{14-18}, repeat from † to † once, K5{7-9}.

Rnd 22: P5{7-9}, K 11, (P5, K 11) twice, P 10{14-18}, K 11, (P5, K 11) twice, P5{7-9}.

Rnd 23: K6{8-10}, † YO, SSK, K5, K2 tog, (YO, K7, YO, SSK, K5, K2 tog) twice, YO †, K 12{16-20}, repeat from † to † once, K6{8-10}.

Instructions continued on page 16.

Rnd 24: P6{8-10}, K9, (P7, K9) twice, P 12{16-20}, K9, (P7, K9) twice, P6{8-10}.

Rnd 25: K7{9-11}, † YO, SSK, K3, K2 tog, (YO, K9, YO, SSK, K3, K2 tog) twice, YO †, K 14{18-22}, repeat from † to † once, K7{9-11}.

Rnd 26: P7{9-11}, K7, (P9, K7) twice, P 14{18-22}, K7, (P9, K7) twice, P7{9-11}.

Rnd 27: K8{10-12}, † YO, SSK, K1, K2 tog, (YO, K 11, YO, SSK, K1, K2 tog) twice, YO †, K 16{20-24}, repeat from † to † once, K8{10-12}.

Rnd 28: P8{10-12}, K5, (P 11, K5) twice, P 16{20-24}, K5, (P 11, K5) twice, P8{10-12}.

Rnd 29: K9{11-13}, † YO, slip 1, K2 tog, PSSO, (YO, K 13, YO, slip 1, K2 tog, PSSO) twice, YO †, K 18{22-26}, repeat from † to † once, K9{11-13}.

Rnd 30: Purl around.

Rnd 31: Knit around.

Rnd 32: Purl around.

Rnds 33-39: Knit around.

Rnd 40: Purl around.

Rnd 41: (YO, K2 tog) around.

Rnd 42: Purl around.

Rnd 43: Knit around.

Rnd 44: Purl around.

Bind off all sts **loosely** in **knit**.

SLEEVE

Slip sts from first st holder onto circular needle.

Cast on 4 sts onto first double pointed needle for underarm; with same needle, K9{11-11} from circular needle; with second double pointed needle, K 14 from circular needle; with third double pointed needle, K9{11-11} from circular needle, **turn**, add on 4 sts for underarm, **turn**, place marker to mark beginning of rnd: 40{44-44} sts total.

Knit around for 4{6-8} rnds.

Decrease Rnd: K1, SSK, knit around to last 3 sts, K2 tog, K1: 38{42-42} sts.

Continue to decrease 2 sts in same manner, every 4{6-8} rnds, 5{5-4} times: 28{32-34} sts.

Work even until Sleeve measures approximately $5^1/_2\{8^1/_2\text{-}10\}$"/14{21.5-25.5} cm from Dividing Rnd.

Next Rnd: [K4{5-6}, K2 tog] 4 times, K4{4-2}: 24{28-30} sts.

CUFF

Rnd 1: Purl around.

Rnd 2: Knit around.

Repeat Rnds 1 and 2 until Cuff measures approximately 2" (5 cm), ending by working a **purl** rnd.

Bind off all sts **loosely** in **knit**.

Repeat for second Sleeve.

FINISHING

Sew sts at underarm together.

General Instructions

ABBREVIATIONS

cm	centimeters
K	knit
M1	make one
mm	millimeters
P	purl
PSSO	pass slipped stitch over
Rnd(s)	Round(s)
SSK	slip, slip, knit
st(s)	stitch(es)
tog	together
YO	yarn over

★ — work instructions following ★ as **many more** times as indicated in addition to the first time.

† to † — work all instructions from first † to second † **as many** times as specified.

( ) or **[ ]** — work enclosed instructions **as many** times as specified by the number immediately following **or** work all enclosed instructions in the stitch or space indicated **or** contains explanatory remarks.

colon (:) — the number(s) given after a colon at the end of a row or round denote(s) the number of stitches you should have on that row or round.

work even — work without increasing or decreasing in the established pattern.

KNIT TERMINOLOGY		
UNITED STATES		**INTERNATIONAL**
gauge	=	tension
bind off	=	cast off
yarn over (YO)	=	yarn forward (yfwd) **or** yarn around needle (yrn)

Yarn Weight Symbol & Names	SUPER FINE 1	FINE 2	LIGHT 3	MEDIUM 4	BULKY 5	SUPER BULKY 6
Type of Yarns in Category	Sock, Fingering Baby	Sport, Baby	DK, Light Worsted	Worsted, Afghan, Aran	Chunky, Craft, Rug	Bulky, Roving

SKILL LEVELS	
BEGINNER	Projects for first-time knitters using basic knit and purl stitches. Minimal shaping.
EASY	Projects using basic stitches, repetitive stitch patterns, simple color changes, and simple shaping and finishing.
INTERMEDIATE	Projects with a variety of stitches, such as basic cables and lace, simple intarsia, double-pointed needles and knitting in the round needle techniques, mid-level shaping and finishing.
EXPERIENCED	Projects using advanced techniques and stitches, such as short rows, fair isle, more intricate intarsia, cables, lace patterns, and numerous color changes.

KNITTING NEEDLES

U.S.	0	1	2	3	4	5	6	7	8	9	10	10½	11	13	15	17
U.K.	13	12	11	10	9	8	7	6	5	4	3	2	1	00	000	---
Metric - mm	2	2.25	2.75	3.25	3.5	3.75	4	4.5	5	5.5	6	6.5	8	9	10	12.75

GAUGE

Exact gauge is **essential** for proper size. Before beginning your project, make a sample swatch in the yarn and needle specified. After completing the swatch, measure it, counting your stitches and rows carefully. If your swatch is larger or smaller than specified, **make another, changing needle size to get the correct gaug**e. Keep trying until you find the size needles that will give you the specified gauge. Once proper gauge is obtained, measure width of piece approximately every 3" (7.5 cm) to be sure gauge remains consistent.
If you have more rows per inch than specified, use a larger size needle for the purl rows; if fewer, use a smaller size needle for the purl rows.

MARKERS

As a convenience to you, we have used markers to help distinguish the beginning of a pattern or round. Place markers as instructed. You may use purchased markers or tie a length of contrasting color yarn around the needle. When you reach a marker on each round, slip it from the left needle to the right needle; remove it when no longer needed.

YARN OVER

Bring the yarn forward **between** the needles, then back **over** the top of the right hand needle, so that it is now in position to knit the next stitch ***(Fig. 1)***.

Fig. 1

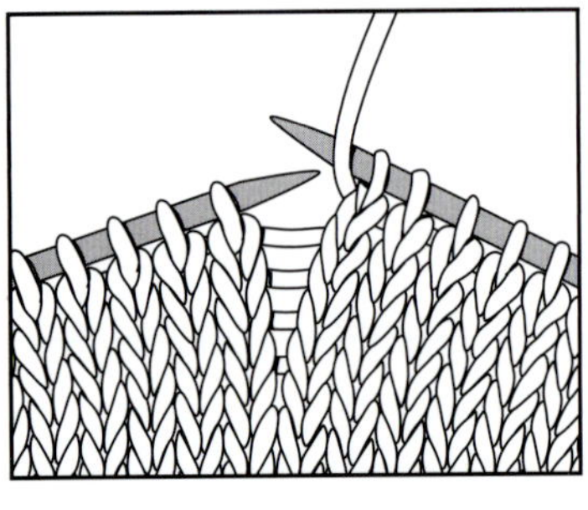

INCREASES

INCREASE

Knit the next stitch but do **not** slip the old stitch off the left needle ***(Fig. 2a)***. Insert the right needle into the **back** loop of the **same** stitch and knit it ***(Fig. 2b)***, then slip the old stitch off the left needle.

Fig. 2a

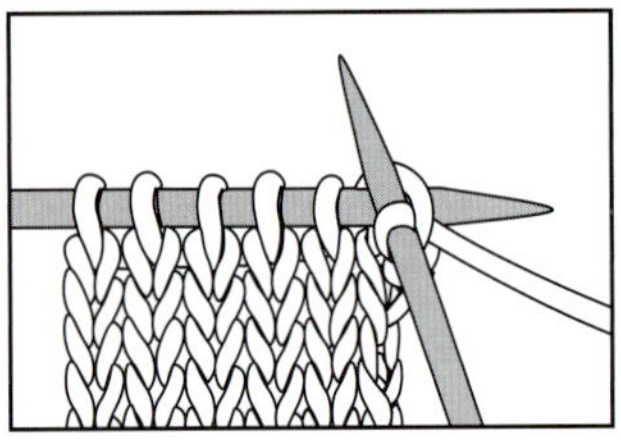

Fig. 2b

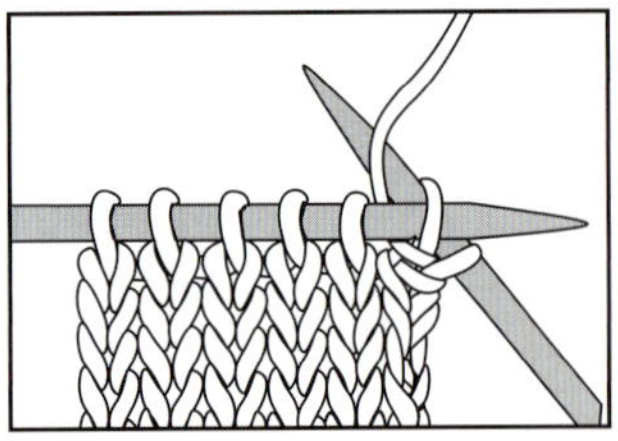

MAKE ONE *(abbreviated M1)*

Insert the **left** needle under the horizontal strand between the stitches from the front ***(Fig. 3a)***. Then knit into the **back** of the strand ***(Fig. 3b)***.

Fig. 3a

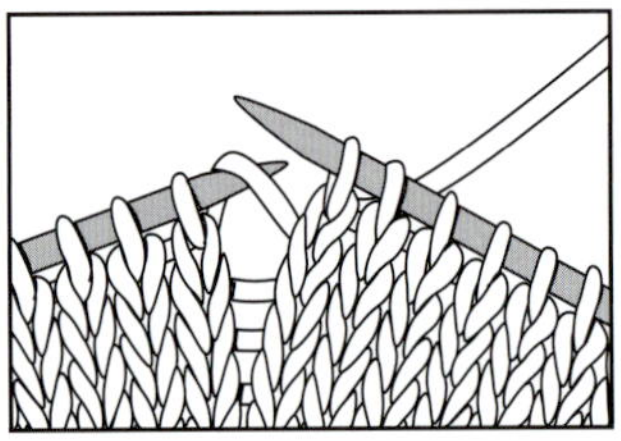

Fig. 3b

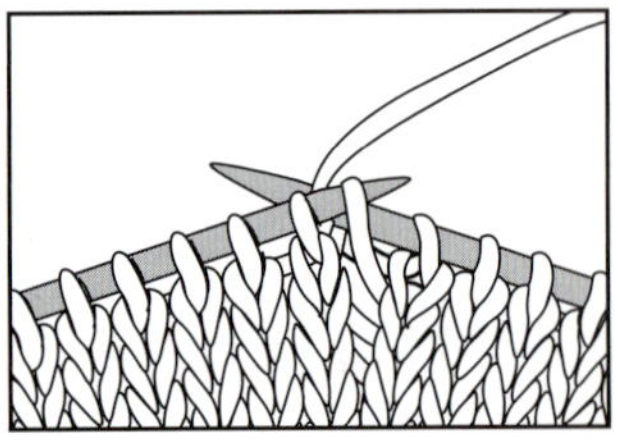

ADDING ON STITCHES

Insert the right needle into stitch as if to **knit**, yarn over and pull loop through ***(Fig. 4a)***, insert the left needle into the loop just worked from **front** to **back** and slip the loop onto the left needle ***(Fig. 4b)***. Repeat for required number of stitches.

Fig. 4a

Fig. 4b

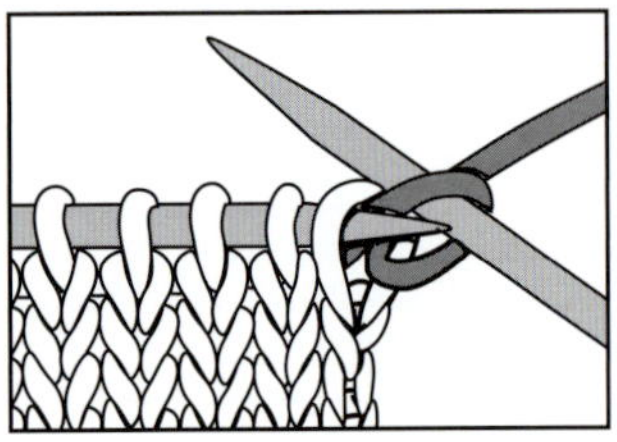

DECREASES

KNIT 2 TOGETHER

(abbreviated K2 tog)

Insert the right needle into the **front** of the first two stitches on the left needle as if to **knit *(Fig. 5)***, then **knit** them together as if they were one stitch.

Fig. 5

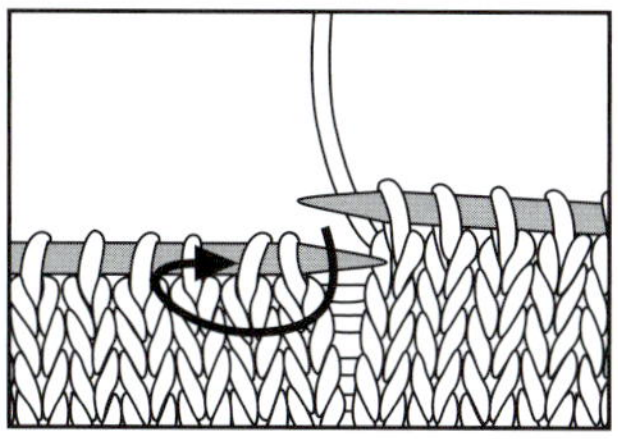

SLIP, SLIP, KNIT

(abbreviated SSK)

Separately slip two stitches as if to **knit *(Fig. 6a)***. Insert the left needle into the **front** of both slipped stitches ***(Fig. 6b)*** and knit them together as if they were one stitch ***(Fig. 6c)***.

Fig. 6a

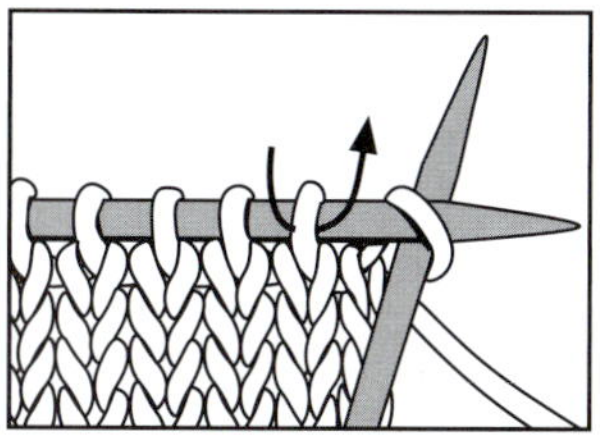

Fig. 6b

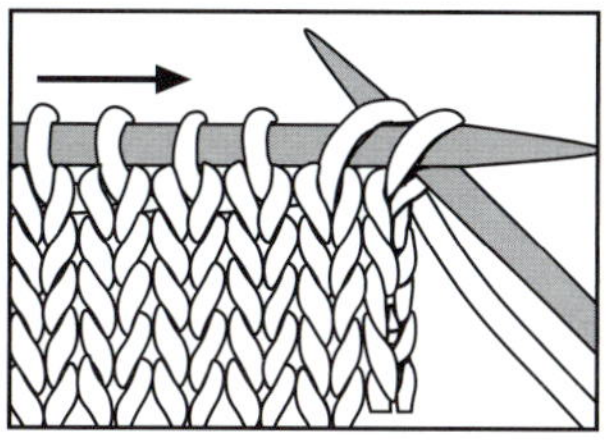

Fig. 6c

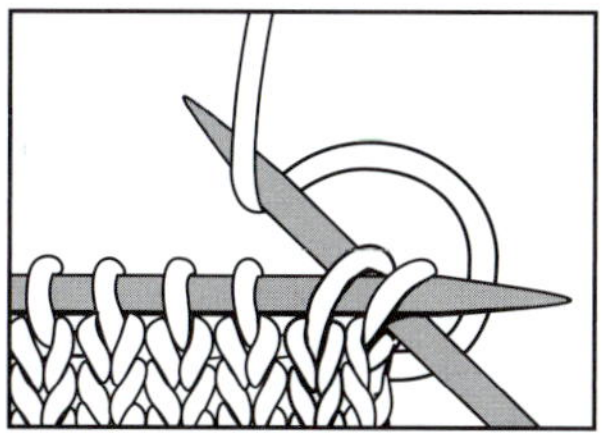

SLIP 1, KNIT 2 TOGETHER, PASS SLIPPED STITCH OVER

(abbreviated slip 1, K2 tog, PSSO)

Slip one stitch as if to **knit *(Fig. 7a)***, then knit the next two stitches together ***(Fig. 5)***. With the left needle, bring the slipped stitch over the stitch just made ***(Fig. 7b)*** and off the needle.

Fig. 7a

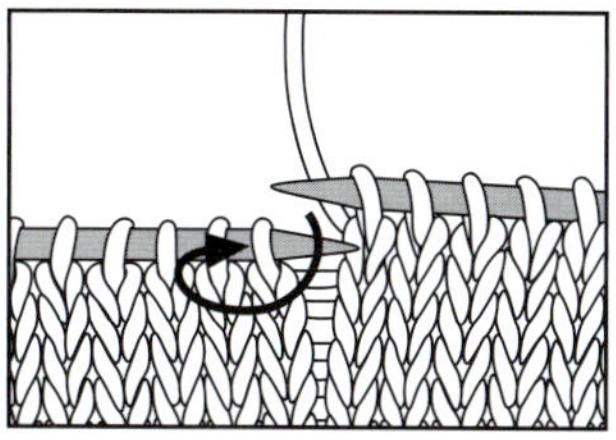

Fig. 7b

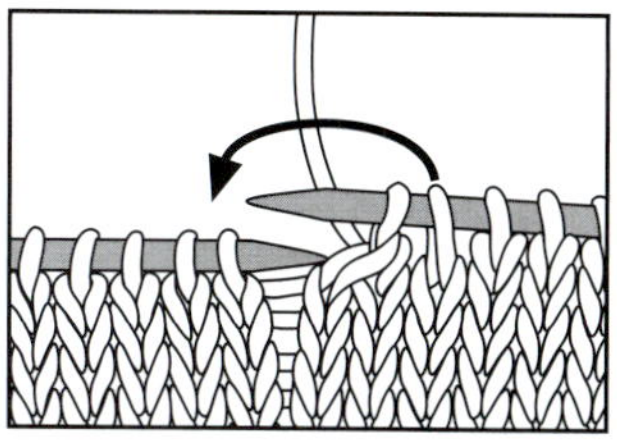

PURL 2 TOGETHER

(abbreviated P2 tog)

Insert the right needle into the **front** of the first two stitches on the left needle as if to **purl *(Fig. 8)***, then **purl** them together as if they were one stitch.

Fig. 8

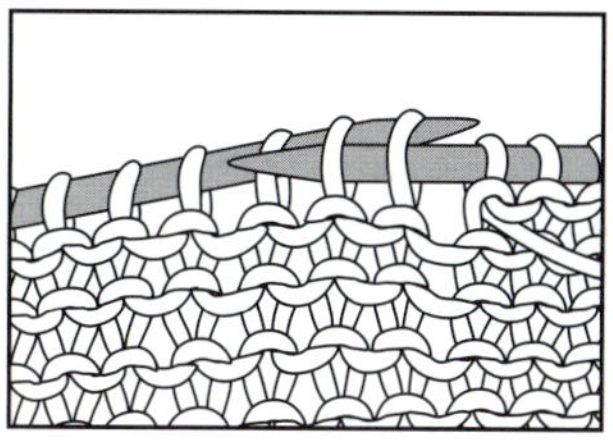

CIRCULAR KNITTING

USING CIRCULAR NEEDLE

When you knit a tube, as for the body of a pullover, you are going to work around on the outside of the circle, with the right side of the knitting facing you. Using a circular needle, cast on all stitches as instructed. Untwist and straighten the stitches on the needle to be sure that the cast on ridge lays on the inside of the needle and never rolls around the needle.

To begin working in the round, knit the stitches on the left hand point ***(Fig. 9)***. Continue working each round as instructed **without turning the work**; but for the first three rounds or so, check to be sure that the cast on edge has not twisted around the needle. If it has, it is impossible to untwist it. The only way to fix this is to rip it out and return to the cast on row.

Fig. 9

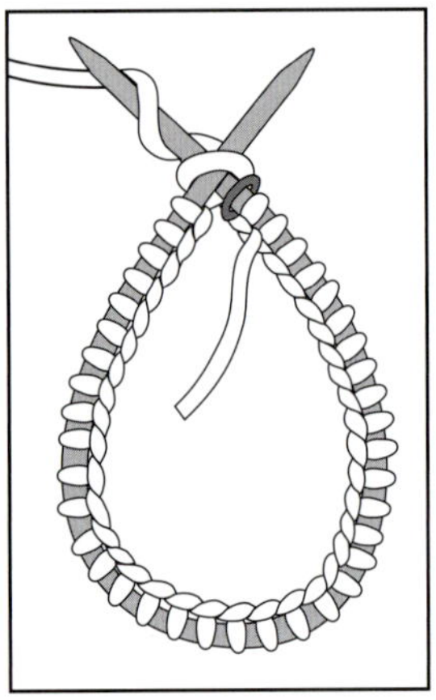

USING DOUBLE POINTED NEEDLES

When working too few stitches to use a circular needle, double pointed needles are required. Divide the stitches into thirds and slip one-third of the stitches onto each of 3 double pointed needles ***(Fig. 10a)***, forming a triangle. With the fourth needle, knit across the stitches on the first needle ***(Fig. 10b)***. You will now have an empty needle with which to knit the stitches from the next needle. Work the first stitch of each needle firmly to prevent gaps.

Fig. 10a

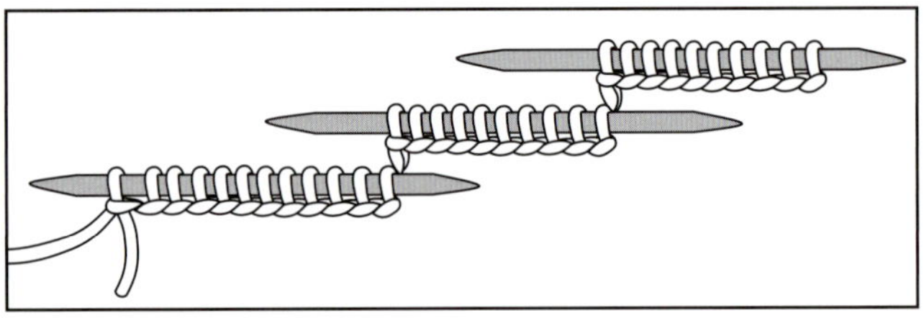

Fig. 10b

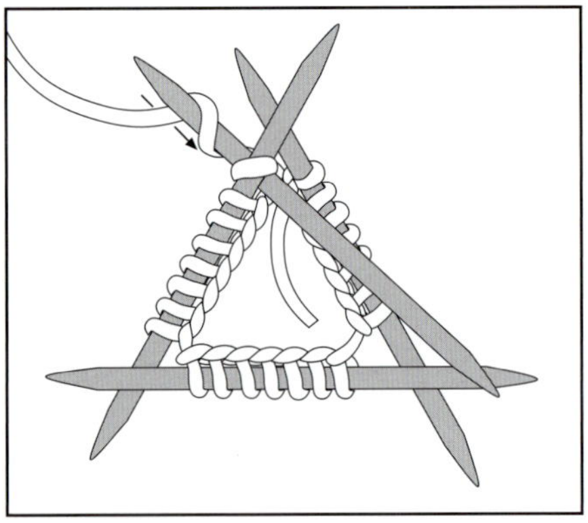